Am I a Priority in Your Life or an Option?

TO: YOGI

Merry X-mas

Am I a Priority in Your Life or an Option?

A Ladies Guide to Understanding Men—
what they don't want you to know!!!

MANSWELL PETERSON SR.

Library of Congress Control Number:		2007907561
ISBN:	Hardcover	978-1-4257-9277-0
	Softcover	978-1-4257-9270-1

To order additional copies of this book, contact:
Xlibris Corporation
1-888-795-4274
www.Xlibris.com
Orders@Xlibris.com
44101

CONTENTS

Never make someone a priority in your life, when you're only an option in Thiers . . . .

This is not a typo . . . . I wanted you to really understand and feel what I am trying to tell you. Go back for a second and let the impact of this statement sink in.

I wrote this book because I had my heart broken by a woman . . . she thought she was over her hurt and pain from a past marriage. She wasn't and she took it out on me, please make sure that your heart is ready to love before you do. To hurt someone because you are hurting is wrong and very, very mean.

DATING

Dating is like shopping for shoes, have you ever bought the first pair you saw? Why . . . there is a selection!!

When I first started to think about this book, a lot of things came to mind. How would I get this point across so that any and everyone that could read and understand this book? It doesn't matter if you are married, divorced, or single, by the time we are finished with this journey together you will have a clear and hopefully better understanding of how a man thinks about different situations. The key word is to listen. Please understand that I am not saying this is the end all . . . and now you will be an expert, but I am willing to bet you won't fall for those pitfalls that your girlfriends talk about all the time. Maybe you have fallen and don't really want to let anyone know that you fell for the craziest game out there. After this is done you will hopefully see where you could have made a turn and avoided the pain and misery that came after you thought you might have found the "ONE".

There are so many ladies out there that are dating and looking for that one that will be their best friend and life partner. Some of you have vowed to not deal with a guy that is not up to standard for what you are looking for. Then ask yourself. Why did I go out with that idiot and why did I stay that long? The question and answer to this is within you. If you get a phone number and you call it several times, but only get a voice mail . . . or better yet the voice mail is full. Here is a clue that something is wrong.

Let's take a look at some examples and show you where the mistake was made and go from there.

You are a successful woman, single or widowed . . . you get the respect at work . . . . you own your home . . . . got the nice car . . . let's say you are divorced (Mind you this applies to all women) this guy sees you and you have been single or by yourself for awhile. Now deep inside you might have been checking out this guy . . . you like the fact that he is cute but don't think he would be a life partner for you. You then make the decision to go out with him . . . hell you have not a date for awhile, it's been so long since you have had sex, Clinton was in office. So you go out with this guy and things actually are pretty cool.

Now this is where your lesson starts, while you think you and him are seeing each other and in the beginning he is spending a lot of time with you . . . . talking on the phone, the two of you go to the movies . . . . he rubs your feet. He even listens to you bitch about how your day was and he does it all with a smile on his face. Now in your head you are thinking . . . WOW!!! This is all I wanted a man that will do all of these things. In his mind, he is putting you in the rotation . . . now you can't go and jump him for this. Women look at things differently than men, he wants to spend time with you and he is also paying close attention to see how you respond to different things in private and public.

Here is an example so it will be even clearer for you . . . . let's use an NFL team for example as you know or don't every team has a starting quarterback with at least two back-ups. The question for you is where do I fit in, more than likely you are not the starter . . . . the woman in this position could have done something to knock herself out of this position and now he is looking to fill the void by cutting her from the team. Don't feel bad about this because this is how you will get to the top. Trust me men and woman do this, it just might be in a different way . . . so lets get back to the team. You are now trying to survive the cut, because I can just about guarantee there are other women looking to survive like you are. Now in his mind he will give each of you time to show and prove yourself. Now I know a lot of you are out there shaking your head . . . saying "I ain't gotta try out for no one's team" YES, you do because dating in a guy's mind is how you will find the one person that you will want to marry or spend the rest of your life with.

Now if you survive this first cut then you will see your time go down just a little. This is what happens when you are spending time with this guy and now it seems he is busy . . . . don't trip, he will be back. Now what you don't realize and can't see is that when you get a quick phone call or a even quicker night time call where all he wants is a piece of you and it's not your heart, and you are happy with this. What is the problem with this? This is a BIG clue that you are not the starter, but you are on the team. Everyone else on the team is getting their time . . . now if he is good he won't cut you off totally, it will just go down a little and he will explain this by saying he is working hard or hanging with the boys. How many work hours are there in one day? HHHMMMM, Ladies there are 24 hours in a day . . . let's say if he works for 8 of them, and sleeps for another 8 . . . what is he doing with the rest of the day!?! And you know he is not spending it with you . . . . Are you starting to get the BIG picture now. Now if you like this guy, you will be happy and suck up all the time he is giving. Think about it like this (Atlanta has a ratio of 17 women to every man) so I know you didn't think you were the only one . . . . plus he plays on the thought you have about your "ME" time . . . . now you really don't give it a second thought. So he is out and about hanging with the other team members seeing which one does what and comparing all of you . . . . sometimes this can be very tiring so there are times when he comes back to you . . . he just wants to chill and snuggle with you. He is now not wasting any energy and you are loving the fact that he is comfortable enough to fall asleep on your couch.

HAHAHAH, well now you know. When his level of energy is up to par again you have snuggle and you are feeling warm to him cause he is "yo" man and BAM you give up the cookies. You are still trying out. He is seeing how needy you are, he is also seeing how much you will trip out on him because he is not around all the time. This process will go on for months sometimes even years, because most women would rather have a piece of a man then none at all. All the while if you are still seeing him that means you are really doing good and your stock is going up. The other women aren't as lucky as they well be benched for you or you might trade spots with them . . . . now you have gotten to the starter position in his life . . . . this is where it is tricky cause now you have his attention almost . . . he is there more now and he will even change his time line of events to cater to you and the things you like to do. He is still banking on the fact that you will need your "ME" time or hang with your girlfriends. Now as you may know already . . . . guys don't dump our friends (Male) because we got a girl. Women will dump everything because they got a man . . . . heck their own mothers fall to the rear. Now you have started to live your life in his world, but he won't do the same for you. You get pissed because you will cancel "Girls night out" to be with him and he is telling you to go, but your needy self wants to be under him. WHY? You should live your life in part time with him . . . . now he knows he got you . . . a fight comes and he hits you with the words "Just because you gave up your friends doesn't mean I have to do the same"

Now you feel like an ass because you have dismissed your girls and you got no one to talk to about him. You feel lost, hurt and betrayed. What you have done is just opened the door for another female to get the guy, you thought it was cool just a few days ago. You have a choice swallow your pride and try to fix this or you could lose him. Think about it this way, there are plenty of good, fine women out there. How many GOOD men are there? There are so many of you . . . . you think because you have the good body and sex, job, house, car, and you can do that trick with your mouth that you could lock us down? NOPE, there are plenty of women looking and you know, women play the game better, but for some reason now . . . . you ladies are really losing your touch. Especially the women over 40, never been married, this group is really feeling the crunch if you have not been married and have no kids. Now the ones that do have kids and are divorced or never been married are just as bad off, when it comes to dating. You think you have it all figured out . . . . I hear women all the time talking about how you gonna change a man. News flash ladies, if he was like that in the beginning, trust me he will be that way in the end.

The really funny thing about trying to 'whip' a guy with your cookies is that, while you might be the bomb in bed . . . . having a guy speaking in tongues' and all. When it is over, it is over. He will lay there and think about how good you were, but it won't keep him there. A lot of women take this approach . . . I know, I know you don't try this . . . . yeah right you have tried it and may not have worked.

This is that moment now where you feel all men are dogs and go to hell. Don't be mad, no one made you do anything you didn't want to. You have to blame yourself, like I said earlier you can get back on the horse and try to ride again or you can just walk off into the dating sunset.

Remember that the guy had other options and while he might miss you for a minute you are about to be replaced . . . . so you can go back and try to fix what is broken or you can just be PISSED. Either way the guy has moved on to the next woman. You and he could have worked out for the long run.

Now you walk around pissed and can't even think right because you feel as though he used you and your cookies. Well first off no one told you to give him the cookies that fast. So now when you see him you see red, and you can't understand why he isn't hurting and pissed cause the relationship didn't work

Let's look at some rules that I have seen or heard from women when it comes to dating.

1. The three month rule—stop watching television, you are a grown ass woman. No one can or should tell you when and how to give your cookies away. I know I just said earlier that you should not get mad at him because you gave it to him and now he has left you alone. That might not be the reason he left you in the first place. It could be that bad ass attitude that you have

2. He can't come over to my place, if my kids live with me.

    Ok, this is a no brainer. I agree with this whole-heartly, but remember this. Why would you even date a guy that's not good enough to meet your kids? Some of you have done this. Now think to yourself for a minute . . . if he is not good enough for my kids, he damn sho ain't good enough to be with me. Doing this will eliminate a lot of the wrong type of baggage that you might see as eye-candy. I am not saying don't have a life, but you can clearly see how this example will fit a lot of single moms. I am a divorced dad, so I know how you feel. If my little one can't meet you, I ask why I am even fooling with you. This could be to see what type of person they are . . . . but you find out very fast . . . . so why waste your time. Please take your time with this one, I am not saying rush him to meet the kids cause you might scare him off ok

3. He got to make this amount of money

Now this one can have you by yourself for the next 20 to 30 years and since some are in their late 30's or 40's that's not good. In today workplace a lot of women make more than the men they might date . . . . at the same time you could be passing by the "Blue-Collar" worker that could be the best man for you. Stop looking at the bottom line and look at your heart. So many of you have passed up a good man, because you felt he didn't make enough money. My all time favorite is the lady that has found a good man, but all of her girlfriends who don't have a man . . . tell you not to date this one. Girl he ain't even on your level. My question for you is do you want to be happy or not.

4. He got to dress a certain way for me to even talk to him.

The funny thing about this is that while you might spend loads and loads of money on your clothes and jewelry. Even more on your shoes, he might not . . . . does that make him a bad person. Some of the best men have been fixed-up by the women they are dating. It could be as simple as showing him where to go and buy nicer things and how to bargain shop, but look his best.

As you can clearly see, there are many factors to dating and we haven't even scratched the surface yet. This chapter will make more and more sense as you go thru this book . . . .

But before we go on . . . . think about something. What is wrong with you talking to more than one man, just like we do when it comes to women? I will tell you one problem; you ladies tell your girls, who will tell their man. Some times silence in what you are doing is the best thing in life. Now this man will tell his boy you are getting played. How are you going to know he is the one if you don't sample more than one. Now don't get me wrong I didn't say you had to go out there and throw yourself on every man.

When you start talking . . . do more listening, this will help you get a better understanding of what this man is all about. Most

(I said most) woman when they go on a date will start to talk and keep going and going . . . . To us your conversation starts to sound like this

Blah, blah, blah, blah, blah give yourself time to take a breath and let us respond to what you just said . . . please remember that I said some. Now some of you it is like pulling teeth when we try to get you to open up and talk. If you are having problems with this, start on the phone . . . this way you are use to talking to him. If you become an introvert it could be a turn off. So sometimes when you are playing that hard to get lady, we will help you out and let you stay hard to get.

ROMANCE

Dead Romance is like having a new car without gas . . . it looks good, but you are not going anywhere.

This is a section that means a lot to women. It doesn't matter what your age is or where you live. When it comes down to romance . . . some guys have it and some don't. You might find yourself in a situation where that is what you need in your life and can't seem to buy it with all the money you might be making. For the guys, we look at this as doing something that will appease you. Now don't get me wrong there are plenty of guys out there that are romantics and love to do the things that make you get chill bumps . . . . you know the kind of stuff that you can't wait to tell your girlfriends about.

Think about this, how many times have you dated a guy and he started doing these things in the beginning. Now you can't get him to do anything like he used to do, before you start fussing or pulling a 'waiting to exhale' moment on him by throwing out his stuff. Ask yourself, what have I stop doing. A lot of times guys will stop doing things because you stopped as well. It can be seen as "The chase is over" it is up to you to keep this fire.

Romance is essential to Love and yes they do go hand in hand. It's like buying a new car and not putting oil in it. It will run for awhile, you will get where you need to go and it looks good when you clean it up. Now since you don't change the oil, you got problems . . . you start to hear the knocking (fights over silly things). Now that you have this problem, what are you going to do? You have to have some major engine work done on this car, and it's going to cost you a lot of money. The same goes for romance in dating and life. Lets look from the other side, the lady that takes her car in for oil changes and to have her tires rotated will not incur have the problems . . . they will come but it wont kill her pocket book at the same time. When you are seeing Mr. Right or you think he is, you have right and a duty to make sure that he understands the things you want and need in a relationship. If you do not put this out there, he will give you the basics and it will be alright at first then you will get tired of this and get pissed. Then he will hear you breathing hard or sighing, then he will ask you what's wrong and you will say nothing. All guys know this is a lie but if we push, then we might get hit with a hell storm. Trust me, not one guy I know wants that to come.

While you are setting up your romantic night with your guy here are a couple of things to check on so you won't be mad if it doesn't turn out like you want it to.

First and foremost, did you check with him to see how his day is planned, does he plan on coming over, is he working late, does he even feel like having company. Now you don't have to tell him what you got planned, but these are very important . . . also you might want to let him know if you are cooking and try to get a time when he might show up. You do not want to go thru cooking a meal and getting desert ready and don't tell him, then he goes and grabs a burger on the way because you never cook. Whatever you do don't drop hints; guys don't pick up hints all the time like you ladies do. This will be a major mistake on your part and then what happens . . . you get pissed because you spent 3 hours cooking and then you went shopping for a sexy outfit to wear for him. Now all of this is blown because you threw hints at him, instead of telling him directly that you had something special planned, don't get anything to eat . . . I got that covered you just bring your appetite and I will take care of the rest. Again get a time estimate it is very important . . . plus by stating this two or more times it lets him know he needs to be there by that time.

Now the physical side is tricky and crazy. You might have been in a relationship where the guy dominated and told you what he wanted and expected you to do this. At the same time he told you what he would NOT do. It is at this moment you have to show your aggressive side, if he wants this, this, and that. Then you should get what you want. Why would you sit there and he is enjoying everything he wants and you are counting ceiling tiles, I have never really understood this one. Once again I know there are the women out there who take charge in this category but for the most they won't say anything . . . . cause they got a man now. Girl stop, you have every right to be pleased as we are, but we just come right out and say what we want. If you want him to take a trip downtown (hopefully you get this one) then you have to tell him. If he does not want to please you in every way, then you might be alright at first because you are thinking Hell I just got him, I don't want to chase him away, he so fine, I am not going to rock the boat. Yet, you sit there in misery because you are not pleased physically, now this will take a toll on you mentally. In time you will keep this bottled up and you will pop, you just don't know when.

Now the funny thing about this is that if 'You' loved yourself like you should you would have checked this from the moment he said this and trust me you would have seen a difference. Think about it this way, a guy will try you to see how much he can do and how much he can get away with. If you don't stop him he will keep going. Remember to always love yourself first and you will have the confidence to tell your man anything at anytime. It is better to get it out than to hold it in and blow up over something so small. The reason you blew up was the fact that he didn't listen, NO that's not it, you are mad because your needs are not being met and you have no one to vent to. Remember you put your girlfriends on the back burner because you got a man. You can't go back and tell them the man that you put them down for is not all that.

Look ladies if you want him to please you in every way tell him. If that man can't make you think about him coming back and tearing your ass up again, something didn't happen right. While I know that there are guys who will never get the second chance. If you like him you should be very verbal and let him know. Also understand this, you know how sensitive your body is tell him where and even guide him there. This is one of those things that will turn him on if he is really into you, if not he is not going to care and you have your answer to how this should go. He will beat up your lower body like a savage and think he is doing something, most just don't care . . . they are thinking she didn't complain so I will do that again. Why go thru years of not be satisfied. Take your time with him and let him know you expect the same.

Days and months go by . . . . now the two of you don't hold hands. The kissing had just about vanished, ask yourself if you are this unhappy what's wrong? He seems like he is just a happy little camper. He is happy because he is getting his, you're the one that is not satisfied. So he is happy and your not. Every time he comes over the first thing on his mind is getting some more. You can put a stop to this, by one having a back up yourself . . . you should have never put all your eggs in that one basket without knowing where it is going and how it will be later in the relationship. Once again he kept more than one in a rotation, plus he didn't let go of his friends.

Anytime you are dealing with a new guy and the two of you are about to do the do, Make sure the playing field is level. If he wants you to wear that Victoria Secret . . . get equal value. Make sure that the spice is given; make sure he takes his time. If you let him jump in and go right to work, the most important part has just been skipped and trust me most guys are going to test you to see if they can skip the touching and kissing. This is the part where you get yourself ready to become one with him. Guys can get the same pleasure by skipping and jumping head first, they won't care if you don't make them. Then some will try to make this as quick as a trip to the convenient store. At this time you need to Stop him and demand he makes you feel like a lady. Not some 10 dollar hooker.(Note: not all guys rush) If you do this trust me, in the end you will have your romantic needs met and it won't become a chore to him, he will like pleasing you in every way. Now on the flip side if you want him to do you, and you don't want to do him . . . . every problem I just told you about will still come, except you will hear about it and if you don't fix it, he will find a woman who will.

Don't get a moment of lust mixed up with romance, trust me they are totally different. If you let a man lust after you, he will never look to love you or romance you in any shape, form, or fashion.

Ladies if you don't have time to fully give your best then don't expect a lot of a romantic situation. Let's call this time exactly what it is a booty call. If you want him to romance you, then tell him. Make him crave you, desire you, want to taste you. Hell, make him want the entire meal, not just a snack.

Body Language

Sometimes God allows suffering in order to get our attention: to divert us from wrong paths; to build our faith and our courage, to help us grow strong and resilient; to make us wiser.

Ladies, ladies, ladies here comes the one. When it comes to body language, you should become a detective. Watch his mannerism and you will pick up so much about how he is feeling and what mood he is in. Now this topic will help also with the romance. Once you start with this for the most part it will be fine.

If he had a bad day at work, you can learn how to flip the script and turn his bad energy into good energy. Think about it this way, you are horny but don't want the touchy feely mood. You want him to go to war with your body and win. There are times when this can be the best cause you will give a release (Pun intended) to get out the frustration that he has and in turn get your freak on at the same time.

There are rules however, if this guy you like/love so much does not care about his outer appearance it is telling you something. I am not saying that he will be clean all the time, cause hell you might date a mechanic and his hands are always dirty. Now if he works in office or in the shop . . . make sure he takes care of himself. If his feet can cut thru your sheets take his ass to the nail shop. This should be a deal breaker; once he realizes this he will change this or ask you to do it for him. There is nothing wrong with a clean cut guy. You also want to make sure he takes care of everything, he should smell good, nice haircut as well. One of the biggest problems is that a woman will chose a guy that doesn't care about these things and get mad cause he won't change. LADIES you can not change him. He has to want to change. In time all men go thru this, some catch on early in their lives and some get it when they become 40 plus. The reason why I put this under this section is body language leads to a lot of romantic times and if he is turning you off, tell he so can fix it . . . it might come down to him asking you, then you can jump in and help him. Only do this if he asks for your help.

Listen to his conversation; if he can't keep a decent topic going then you will one day get fed up with this. A guy that is interested in you can keep a smooth flow to a topic with you and you both go back and forth with no problems. Now if this can't happen and if you are a talker this will blow up one day. The best part about communication is that is happens without a struggle.

So now if this is coming about and he doesn't smell good and can't talk past a tenth grade level, why are you even entertaining this guy if you have a masters. Hopefully you will get this, I am not saying down a guy because he is not on your level, there are plenty of guys who never went to college and can hold their own when it comes to any topic. I am just saying make sure that you find one that fits you.

If you are trying to get close to him and your touching him and you get no response from him, that is a tell-tell sign. He might not be in the mood or something is on his mind. Now if you push this you might get your stuff crammed in and feel used. If you try and talk then he might let you in. I know you're asking what if he won't let me in, what do I do then? Simple you wait; most guys will figure it out and come out of this mood soon.

If you are calling him and he doesn't answer the phone every time you call, it's not that he doesn't want to talk to you. He might be busy; this is funny because now you have just given him your power. Now you are sitting back and waiting for his return phone call. You have a life, so start living it. Don't be sitting there by your caller ID waiting for his name to pop up. It might be hours or even a day or two before he calls back. Now you are sitting there pissed. Don't ever do this ladies, if you call him and don't answer and you leave him a message and he doesn't call you back in an hour. Don't call him back every two hours . . . how many of you have done this. Now he really knows you want his attention and will use this against you. You can't see it but trust me, he does.

You and your man have been seeing each other for a couple of months now, and sometimes he throws it down in bedroom. Here lately he is not doing it. What's missing? Are you still doing your part, remember that you are still in competing with other females out there for his attention. Yes, I said it. Trust me; just like you were looking for a man, they are too. The sad thing is that in some areas like Atlanta the ration of females to males is 17 to 1. So just because you got him and he is spending time with you, that doesn't mean the game is over. That just means that you have to step up even more. Now I know a lot of you are saying . . . WAIT that's a two way street. No it is not . . . . it is like supply and demand. The demand is up for a good man; sorry but this is the sad truth.

So think about it, how about that surprise when he comes over . . . . something nice and silky or better yet almost nothing to really get his mind off of every thing out there. You're body gives a vibe, some of you know this. Others don't, while you are saying I got my man. There is some female also looking at him and saying I am going to get him. Life is not fair and neither is dating.

You can really tell a guy is into you when there are times when he can't keep his hands off of you. But here is something that might mess you up, you can also tell when he wants to hold you, touch you and his mind is farther from sex than you can imagine. Just the presence of you around him gives him joy. He might want to cook with you; he might watch your favorite television show with you. He might invite you to watch his. That simple hug that he gives or that smile to let you know he still likes what he sees. So while you decide to give up your girls and your routine of going to the gym, now all that food and the happiness of love in the air is showing by you not being able to wear your clothes anymore. If you notice he is still going to the gym and hanging with his fellows, why are you not going to girl's nights out and the gym?

He wants to miss you; I know I know I told you about the other women. Listen when he sees you are a well rounded woman, not in fat cells, he will want more of your time. Don't get this statement twisted, some guys like big girls too. You will see him structure it to where he can be around more. He still does his thing and you should do it to, this gives him time to miss you. Now when you go away, that doesn't mean call him every half-hour to see where he is at or when is he coming over. If you come across as to needy then you can chase him right into the arms of the woman that does not need him every free hour that he has. A simple text message to make him smile or a quick call to let him know you miss him, which is all that is needed trust me this works. Think about it, if he is going to cheat . . . you can not stop this. That's why you have to have a life outside of what you have with him, and if he is caught cheating you can tell him to kick rocks and your life will go on. You will hurt for a moment, but you got your girls there for support and you don't have to hear a lot of I told you 'so' from them because you dumped them. Don't dump them and they will be there for you.

When you go to buy a pair of shoes, you try on several pairs—right? Right, so you have to do a trail and error with this, to find out what really works. Remember you don't want to come off as desperate, but confident. This will pull him into whatever mood that you are feeling.

Don't read
between the lines

The ability to read and understand what you just read is Wisdom.

When it comes to talking and listening ladies you don't give guys enough credit. There are times when we actually hear you. We might not always let you know that we hear and understand what you are trying to get across to us, but trust me we hear you. The biggest problem is that you don't hear us. We can ignore you for several reasons: either we don't want to admit you are right about a subject or simply we don't want to hear you rant and rave about the subject. This will drive a man crazy . . . if you are right smile inside and let it go. Some of you do this way past the point of right or wrong . . . you do it so much we disappear for some time, just not to hear your mouth.

Now if you have a man that doesn't like to talk, email or text. You have a major problem. If he tells you this from the start, then you have to make a decision whether you can deal with this or not. Sometimes this can make things very uncomfortable. Especially if you love to talk or have some form of communication. Men are cut and dry with this, either you will have a man who enjoys talking or one that doesn't. Find out which he likes to get his message across and use this, but be forewarned if you over do this . . . he will start to ignore you and all of your messages. Now if he does respond to you in any form, make sure you respond back . . . but don't write a book, after 50 to 100 words you have lost him and now he is scanning. This is why you can come back later and say remember when we talked about this and he looks at you like you are crazy.

How many times have you been talking to a guy and he will tell you he is not looking for a relationship and you thought he has everything you are missing. Your thought process goes on to say I bet I can make him my man. Now if you would have listened to what he just told you, you would have heard him the first time.

Maybe this will get you thinking, how many of you have done this or had your girlfriends do this. You meet a "good" man and you start thinking of him as yours and in your mind you start thinking about the two of you getting married and what the kids would be like . . . what kind of house you think the two of you would need. Now this guy is just meeting you and he has not had any thoughts close to what is going thru your mind.

You ask the guy about kids and he tells you "I don't know" this doesn't mean start thinking if you get some or you have some that he is cool with kids. He merely said he doesn't know. You have to consider if he wants kids or if he already has children.

If you and this guy are talking about the big "L" word—LOVE and he goes to Texas just to get to Florida and you are in Georgia, he is telling you that he doesn't feel this way about you. Now don't get me wrong, it is not saying that he couldn't love you, but at this moment in his life he doesn't love you. Now if you keep pushing he will eventually break down and say this just to appease you and he really doesn't mean it at all. Later you are crushed because you find out how much he really doesn't love you.

Ask yourself would you want a guy to love you and he knows it from his heart to that crazy feeling he gets in his stomach or do you want it to be pressurized from you and it really holds no meaning to him at all. Ladies you tend to lead with your heart on your sleeve and your forehead. This can be very dangerous, because you will have guys out there just telling you things just to get into your bedroom.

Just because he said "I Love You" does he really mean it? He will tell you in the little things that he does or doesn't do for you. There are too many Television shows and magazines telling you what love is . . . this is something that you have to figure out for yourselves. If he is not responding to you the way you think he should he is telling you that he likes you and he likes where he is right now.

This type of reading the lines that are given to you will tell you everything that he wants you to know. Remember actions speaks louder than words, so when he says that he cares for you—he didn't say "I Love You". Many of you jump the gun when you hear a guy say anything close to love. Don't do this, he is clearly telling you he likes you and the time you are spending.

The pressure many guys feel is that the closer some of you get to that biological clock, the more desperate you are to have kids. Don't give off these signs, if a guy sees that you are mad, horny for some kids of your own—he will run for the hills and leave you choking in his dust. For the ones of you with kids, be selective and chose guys that will be nice enough for your kids to meet them one day. Now I didn't say meet him today, and next week he is meeting the kids, mom, dad and Uncle Joe. No what I am saying is give yourself enough options so that if something goes wrong, you have a back-up plan.

If a guy tells you this and I am sure a lot of you have heard this one . . . "I'll call you later" look at what he said, he said I will call you later . . . or he might have said I will talk to you later. This does not mean he will call you back that same day. Now if you want to clarify then you need to ask him. It doesn't hurt to make him commit to a time . . . such as "Around what time today are you going to call, because I have to step out" now what you have just done is to let him know that you have an interest in him but you will not leave that open to any misunderstanding. Once you do this . . . . listen to his voice change because he is not ready for this he will give you a time and will make sure to do this, if he cans. Remember there might be other commitments he has to take care of. What you are doing is demanding your time and letting him know at the same time that I will not be over-looked or played with.

At this time he is now thinking and wondering how to rearrange his times to make that call to you. Now when he does call, try to keep him on the phone for a bit, this throws a monkey wrench in his game, because he was planning on calling you then coming up with some reason why he can't stay on the phone.

See at this point he is telling you that you are important enough to give that required time, and he sees you want your time and will not be put on the back-burner.

If he doesn't call, then he is telling you I was too busy to give you a ten minute phone conversation. Now what you have to do to off set this, the next time he calls you don't answer the phone. This part is very important because now he will see your time is important to you and that you are not sitting by that phone waiting on him. Most of you won't do this; this is why the guy can control every bit of the time he spends with you

Now here comes the big one!!! If the guy you are seeing gives you a key to his place . . . please understand that he is giving you the rope to hang yourself with. Your asking yourself, why is that. He loves me or likes me enough to give me access to him and his place; he isn't doing it to test me. OH HELL YES HE IS!!!! At first you won't think this but as we go on further you will see. Now at this point he is seeing just how far you will go to find out about any other women he may or may not be in contact with. This is where most women lose it and become free agents because he kicks you completely out of his life.

Now think about it, the key is to get into his place, he gave you this gesture so that if you are off work before him you can come over and chill. Sometimes he might get caught in traffic and he doesn't want you sitting in your car waiting on him to get to his place. This is what it appears to be and for the most part it is true, he is more accepting of you in his personal space. Most women love this, because they now have that inside access. Believe it or not a large majority of you ladies will blow this within six months of getting that key. It called the 'snoop' factor, you just have to be nosey and look around to get a better feeling of him and what he might be doing. Most of you still believe that he still might be doing something on the side. I know, I know you wouldn't do this . . . . yeah right (once again). Now some of you are smart, you might find something and never bring it up, but some of you will call him on anything that you might find.

Here is an example of what I am talking about; I gave a lady a key to my place one time and I left out a cruise package that I had taken about 4 months prior, just to see if she would snoop and find it. Now mind you this trip was taking months before but I also placed it under some other papers on my desk. Now the only way she could have found it was to be 'snooping' . . . . she almost got away with it, but she couldn't resist asking me about taking a trip one day. I didn't respond like she wanted and she got mad, she then threw it up in my face that I took a trip with so and so, why wasn't she good enough to go on a trip with. BAM, she was busted . . . she held it for about two months. When I asked her about what she was talking about, she went right back to my desk and found the information. I told her about the trip, but I also schooled her on looking at everything, the trip was before her and just because I went on a trip, that doesn't give her the right to question it. Now once again I know, I know you wouldn't do this. While I will agree women can get away with more this is not for the perfect woman who has everything on lock down. This is clearly for the ones of you that can't seem to figure why every time you think you have reached a point with a man something goes wrong.

See in the above example, just like women test men, we test you. If you think about, this is why a lot of men won't open up and tell you everything going on with us because at some time or another you will bring it up in our faces . . . like in a heated argument.

This is why a lot of information is given very, very slowly from a man. During this early process, you really need to listen to him and find out what he is saying. Now if you hit him with a million and one questions he will feel like you are grilling him. In time he will give you all the answers to any questions you might have about him and his past. He will eventually break things down so that you can really understand what he has gone thru. If he has been hurt, he will tell you this. This could be very important if he tells you this, especially if a woman has crushed his heart. He will tell you he is not looking for any thing serious, believe him. It is better to know that right now, he looks at you as a friend not his woman.

A lot of this comes to mind about how a guy feels about certain things as well, if he tells you that he doesn't eat a certain thing. Why would you tell him, "You haven't tried mine yet?" and you will actually fix this dish and expect him to eat it. He clearly was telling you something to save you time and feeling like your heart just got crushed. Now because you didn't listen you feel as though you just wasted your time and money. If you would have taken his word, this would not have happened.

Another example is that when you meet a guy and finally get over to his place, don't start decorating it in your mind. Then you start making suggestions as 'I know how to lighten your place up' or why don't you put up this or do that. He will tell you its fine like it is . . . . but you can't accept that, off to Wal-mart you go—with your credit card/debit card in hand. You are going to fix up his place to make you more comfortable there not for him. Some of you might even go as far as to ask what do you like, what colors? He didn't ask you to do none of this, but yet you are doing these things. A lot of you will do this because of the sheer happiness of having a man in your life. Then the moment you feel he has broken your heart, you want all of your stuff back. Well dang no one asked you to do all of this anyway.

MONEY, MONEY, MONEY

When this subject comes in it changes the good people to bad and bad people to good. Think about this very hard and long because once money becomes an issue in your relationship, it might never be the same.

Even if you are the sweetest person in the world, your new attitude can really hit a sour note if you loan money to a boyfriend. He may really need the help and you know that he has a good head on his shoulder, you should always think twice about this.

Let's just say he is struggling and we all know at one point or another I think we have struggled. Don't get the big head and say out loud no I have never struggled; some times karma has a way of catching up with you and can knock you clearly on your behind.

Here you are you have found you a man and now everything is going fine . . . you are hanging out at his place and he is hanging out at yours. He has to change jobs and now his pay period is off. He needs 50.00 to finish paying a bill, what do you do? This is your man, the one you are hanging out with and by spending all this time together you know he has a great heart and he is making progress towards his goals in life. So do you loan him the money or do you give it to him. This is where the trouble lies, because if you can loan it to him without hitting a pothole in your budget that is fine. Now if you loan it to him and he later finds out that it will be two weeks not one week before he gets his first check . . . . how are you going to respond.

Most of you would actually act a plum fool and start ripping him from ear to ear about how you needed the money and it was going toward a bill that you had. Now the old saying . . . . 'Don't kick a horse when he is down' plays a good part here. You should never had loan him the money if you could not go without, but I know that's your sweetie and you saw he needed it. The reason I say don't loan it because now that pressure is on him to make sure that he pays you back quick. There is nothing worse than owing a female money because she is quick to always reference it to you and sometimes not in the right place. Here we go again I hear you, I hear you . . . . I wouldn't do my man like that! How many of you reading the book has done something out of character and knew it wasn't you? How many of you have said something you wish you could take back once it rolled off your tongue? How many of you have talked dirty about the man you once loved with all your heart?

Funny thing is I know now a lot of you are feeling what I am saying . . . . What is even funnier is that the girls you are bragging to about how your man does this or that are sometimes waiting for you to mess up so that they can steal your man . . . . I guess you don't think this happens either huh?

Ok so as you can see it is better to give it and not look for it and tell your man . . . . "Baby when you get it then you can give it back or simply say I just don't have it to give to you.

Now here you go shaking your head saying I shouldn't have to give NO money to a man. So you think that only women struggle, wow!! If this is what your thinking you are farther gone than I thought.

Let's flip the page for a second, let's say it is you that needs the help. I know a lot of you are saying "if I need the help and he is sweet enough to help me out that is fine with me. I mean I am his woman". Well you know what guys think the same way, this applies to all types. It doesn't matter if he is making a good salary, things will happen. But let it be you and you see no harm, plus you might not want to pay it back. (Some of you will run to pay it back)

Let's say that he does not have it to give you or loan you. For any one of several reasons are you going to dump him or cut his time. Some of you go back to a saying that used to be said a lot while I was growing up 'No romance without finance. Now so what you are really saying is that if you can't help me—then there is no need for you to be here. This could be a time where you both are tight with money and he just doesn't have it. A guy that has a true woman that will stick by him thru thick and thin is going to be the one he is with for the long haul. Troubled times don't last always, and just think how many guys did you let go because he couldn't spend money on you. Then will see that person later and they finally go it all together and is happy with another woman. (Yeah I know it happens to us also) but every woman reading this book knows about a friend who has dumped a guy because he wasn't balling as they say)

Since we are on the subject of money, let's look at it this way—you and your man are going out for the evening; he wants to see a movie then grab a bite to eat. He has a place in mind for both but you want to go to a more expensive place. Is it right or wrong for you to demand to go to your selection knowing; he doesn't have enough money or are you willing to say here honey I really want to eat here and give him some extra money so you can be wined and dined like the lady you are. Well for the most part some of you feel as though it is up to the man to pay for everything . . . then some of you feel I can carry my own. It is all in how you present it to him that's makes a difference. If he sees you are a partner then everything is cool, but if he sees you as a controlling woman who demands things, then get ready cause your time with him is about to go away.

SEXUAL ADDICTION AND SCHOOLING DR. THUMB

The best students aren't the ones who get an "A", they are the ones who use their Knowledge to better themselves.

Here is the section the book that most women have really been wondering about. How do you deal with dating after a long marriage or a very long relationship?

This is the point of life you have to be very, very careful. When a guy finds out that you have been off the market and not having sex, let's just say the sharks are coming out of the water.

What I am saying is for the woman who was divorced and she has not dated in 5 years, she has her needs but because she has not been having them met, she is fine. Until she decides to start dating again, now she runs across a guy who has been active in the dating market. So since he is still in regular season form, he has an active sex drive and can go until his body just stops. When this guy and woman actually meet and start dating, she makes the mistake and tells him that she has not been dating and that she has not had sex for several years. In this guys mind bells and whistles start to go off. This happens for several reasons . . . cause he knows now if he ever does get to her and can have sex with her . . . it is a done deal (this is based on the fact that he knows what he is doing) Now they date and the woman's body start to awaken from its long sleep, now she is getting horny but doesn't want to tell the guy. In her mind she is thinking "I am going to kill this guy" In his mind he is thinking "I will have her begging for me"

Who do you think is right in this situation? For the most part I can tell you the guy will win this. No and it's not because I am a guy, it is based on all the previous information I have given you . . . . let's look further.

The relationship (in her mind) and friendship (his mind) start to blossom and they start spending a lot time together. The guy is careful not to push to hard but he makes sure that she knows that she can have him at any given time. In her mind now she is even more excited because he is not pushing to hard for her to have sex. The shark (Guy) knows that if he waits he can have the entire meal and since no one else is even close the meal will be his as long as he doesn't trip himself up.

Now a couple of more weeks go by and he is getting some from some other honey pot . . . . all the while slowly caressing her gentle ego and body at the same time. He calls everyday and he spends time with her on every occasion that he cans . . . he senses the blood is about to be spilled, and sure enough she offers herself to this man. At first he tells her no, he wants her to be sure. This is all part of the trap . . . to show her he really does care about her. She is going crazy . . . she has found a really nice guy.

Now he takes his time and he kisses her all over her body . . . making sure she is being driven crazy at every moment that he gives her . . . . BAM!! The trap has been set and she is caught in it. Now he takes his time and makes love to her for a very long and planned period. She is sent away with the shaky leg syndrome. Now she is smiling from ear to ear and everyone that knows her senses this glow about her and she is bursting at the seam to tell someone about the guy that has turned her world inside out. If she only knew, over the next couple weeks he will do the same and now she is hooked on it . . . he knows that he can disappear and even though she might trip, she will forgive him. He does this because he knows that since it took her so long to get back into the dating game that she is not going to run right out there and pick up another guy. This is what he is banking on. I know right now all the ladies are saying "Damn Dog." So is it his fault that she waited for ever and a day to get back out there. I am not saying this to be mean and cruel, but sometimes you have to get back on that bike and ride again.

So now no matter how mad she gets, she will let him back in because she doesn't want to have to go thru the dating process all over again. Hell, look how long it took for her to get this one. Then she thinks about her girlfriends who were dating and can't find a man so she decides to keep the trifling piece of a man that she has. She thinks to her self than since the pickings are bad, at least she got one that makes her feels good. This is what I meant by the trap you just read about. This man knows about the shortage of decent men and he has taken full advantage of this scenario.

Now this can go for women who are young and older. Once you give a guy this kind of power then he uses it on you every occasion that he can. Now when you think of it, both sides are really getting something out of the deal. He has a woman that will wait for him and she gets to have her fun with him. She starts to feel alive again, and that is why she got back into the dating game to find someone. The only difference is that she was looking for someone to be hers and hers only. Now I am not saying that they won't be together like this . . . because in time he might decide that she is what he wants. There is nothing you ladies can do to make this choice for him. It will have to come from his brain. You can give all the hints and clues.

I have known women to try and make the guy jealous, and had it backfire. So if that is the way your going I warn you to be very careful with that one. Remember earlier when I told you are on a team when the dating game first starts. All you will be doing is making him fire you and then you start back over again. Most good women know their own worth so; most men will come to see that.

Sex is the biggest disadvantage that we have over the ladies . . . I know a lot of you are saying or shaking your heads trying to figure out how can he say that. I will back it up with this . . . . if you have been single for awhile and then you start to have sex on a regular basis. You are comfortable with the man that you have allowed into your body, that's why the first couple of sexual encounters with men are the best . . . he is trying to make a point and with most of you he will make this point.

Now some of you poor ladies have had the unfortunate timing of meeting 'Dr. Thumb' if you know what I mean (A man with a small penis, but did a lot of bragging about what he would do) now when this guy comes at you . . . . he is talking up a storm about what he is going to do to you. Now you really are excited about this and can't wait until he shows you his "Super Powers" now once he shows up he is like Superman . . . walks in with his chest all stuck out and five minutes into handling his business, now he looks like Superman shot in the chest with a shotgun full of kryptonite. All of sudden your super hero is down for the count and then he got a nerve to start snoring with a smile on his face. Now you are sitting there pissed off. You rudely wake his ass up and escort him out of your house. Then head to your bathroom to get your bullet out.

Just for the sake of conversation ladies lets look at it another way. You met a man that's seems to got it all together. Nice house, car, job, but damn he can't please you sexually at all. Do you dismiss him and don't look back or do you try to train him. The scary part about this is that you train him and you guys break up and another woman is enjoying everything that you taught him. Now the good side would be that the two of you make it work, and then your problem is solved.

How many times have you worked with a guy and then once he improves, he moves on to his next victim . . . oops I mean woman . . . . yeah you see what I mean. The only time a relationship is guaranteed is when the married couple is in the ground and buried. No one took your man, he was never yours. The moment you realize this, your healing has begun.

HAVE YOU EVER WONDERED WHY YOU NEVER MET HIS FAMILY/FRIENDS?

A secret is just that. That is why YOU were never revealed!!

Y ou have been kicking it and hanging with your new man for a while. You have told all of your friends about him. You have even mentioned him to some members of your family. Now the curiosity is going in circles in your head as to "Why haven't I met his family or his friends?" Clearly you think "I am a good woman!!"

Now if you are reading this you can clearly go back in this book and it is all making sense now. Damn girl, it took you this long but I am glad you got it!!! You are not the starter, only the starter goes around the family and friends. While this is not a bad thing, but it does clearly show you where you really stand with him.

Have you started to think about all the guys that did this to you? Now of course, some guys won't have any family in the city where you two live. But now the holidays have come and gone, someone's birthday—was it his grandmother, sister, or maybe a brother. Could it have been a family reunion? Now it is really sinking in, and you are pissed, because the guy that you have uplifted to everyone has not been to hardly anything you invited him to. Now you are really mad. This starts to take an immediate effect on you. Damn it, two months ago you had the get-together at your girlfriends' house and you invited him. Maybe it was the office function and you wanted to show him off to your co-workers . . . hell it might have been dinner at your house with a couple of your family and friends and it was the same thing all of the time. He was BUSY!!! And time after time you came up with an excuse for him, your heart was sunk and now after reading this you can clearly see what the hell was really going on.

As I told you earlier in this book and maybe I need to say this louder. YOU ARE NOT THE STARTER. Let me break this down even further for you. Let's say you and your girls are getting together at one of their houses and you invite him, even though this city you are in is/might big, Karma has a way of showing it's ugly little head at the wrong time. What do you think would happen if he showed up with you and one of his other women showed up? Even better, what if one of her girls showed up. Now the two of you have never met, but she knows about her girl who is dating a man with the same name. Now women are very smart, so she gets close ask several questions and gets just enough information to sneak and call her girl. You know girl power and all. She asks her girl what she is up to and then asks if her man is with her, when the answer no comes—all hell with break loose soon. This is when she asks her girlfriend what does he look like, and then she describes him to her girl even giving some features about him. Now this other woman starts to feel sick, because he told her he was hanging with the guys playing poker or something. This other lady might even find a way to sneak a picture using her cell-phone. Now the proof is in the pudding and now the other woman you are competing with is on the way to the party. Now this guys knows the rules and he should have been paying attention to all the ATTENTION this other woman was giving him. She might have been asking one too many questions. If he doesn't exit stage left and quick it will be world war III. This is why most men don't go anywhere with the other women. He only goes and hangs out with the starter, but he will avoid this kind of setting at all cost. He knows that doing this will avoid everything I just told you.

Now you are really shaking your head, because you feel like a damn fool, please don't do this to yourself. This happens all the time, but after guys share stories about how they got caught up at this type of event, most learn and adapt. This is why now, no matter how much you beg and plead for him to come he WON'T.

The funny thing is that they always say women know how to play the game and get away all of this kind of stuff. But guess what, not only now have we caught up with you ladies but I really do believe that we have passed you.

Yes ladies I just said it, here is a bonus one for you. Have you ever wondered why you guy is always cleaning up his place and always have fresh sheets on the bed? NOPE it is not because he is a clean freak . . . it is because the back-up just left hour(s) ago and he just washed all the evidence in the washer. (That was a freebie I know it had nothing to do with it, just wanted you to know)

So now you know why you are a ghost to the family and when they finally do met you. The family has a problem with your name or they are looking at you in shock because they just got used to the other lady with whom they thought he would have married and they all liked her. Has one of these relatives ever called you another ladies name . . . . this is why. Then all of a sudden you say something crazy like . . . "I have heard so much about you" . . . they can't say the same because it's true. They just heard about you a couple of hours or days ago.

But hey, congratulations are in order, you have just been made the starter. Enjoy your time and whatever you do . . . try to keep your spot. (Have you ever paid attention to your passenger side mirror on your car . . . it has a saying on it 'objects in mirror are closer than they appear') remember that you just replaced someone and your competition is right on your heels . . . so do your thang girl. Think about it, you have replaced the last one. Now while you are there and you are feeling good, this is when the mom or dad pulls your man to the side or ask him to come to the kitchen. They want to know what happened to the last one.

DOWN LOW/ IN THE CLOSET GUYS AND REAL MEN

Now this will be sweet and short ladies. Stop thinking that every guy is a down low guy. It is not true.

While they may have hurt your dating prospects and I do mean bad, you have to have an open mind about this. Trust me all the straight guys are frustrated enough with this type of behavior. For one it has all of us on edge, because if you get with one of these guys, how honest are you going to be about being fooled by this idiot.

Not only has he put your life in jeopardy, but he also put ours at risk. If I am sleeping with you and you slept with him then I can get what he gave you. Now I know it will take you awhile to get over this and the hurt is very bad. So don't get mad at me cause he hurt you, hell what you need to do is be going to the free clinic and getting your HIV/AIDS test done every six months to make sure he has not passed anything on to you.

So as you can see, this is scary for us just like it is scary for you. I don' think I need to harp on this too much, you can clearly see how I feel and I really believe that I know how you feel.

SEXUAL APPEAL

What you won't do . . . the other woman will!!!

Ok, now here we go . . . you finally got the man of your dreams or at least you think so. You figure all of your hard work of being so picky has paid off. You no longer have to be in the fight with other woman . . . you have won. Everything I told you about in previous chapters has been mastered. You can finally rest your head, no more having to dress up being sexy for him anymore. Wrong, wrong, wrong, this is when your fight truly begins. Now that you have him, you have to fight harder to keep him. Just as you had to go thru hell to get that man, another woman is still looking for dream guy, and she has your guy in mind.

I know you are saying to yourself . . . . damn, I thought it was over at this point, but it is not. Remember how sexy you got for him . . . making sure that you got that pedicure and manicure. You never let him see your toes not polished . . . or if they were messed up, it wasn't that bad. Well now he is still paying attention, he still wants to see that sexy woman that caught him totally off guard. He wants to see that woman whose scent alone could drive him up a wall, just by you passing by him. You need to flirt even more now. I can see you shaking your head back and forth trying to figure out why, if he loves me—we should be good to go. The only thing that might be good to go is your man. If you come to bed every night wearing that very comfortable big ugly t-shirt . . . you know the one with a couple of holes in it because it just feels so good. You have started back tracking, think about it ladies, how many of you have seen a man not getting treated by the lady in his life, and he is out there looking, I know you are wondering . . . how is he being treated wrong? I still cook . . . hell you might even clean. But it comes with a complete package, which means he wants to see that sexy side of you . . . and not just on the weekend. Now if you only showed this on the weekend from the start, then you are good to go. Now come on . . . dating is not just a weekend deal anymore.

So as you can see men want to see that sexy side of you anytime . . . anyplace. I am not saying you have to do it daily, just enough to keep him wondering. The more you do to keep him on his toes, the more you will get from him. I know you were waiting for this to come up. In your mind you are saying . . . he got to do his part also, while this is true . . . remember that the ratio is in his favor, not yours. Another woman is sitting there waiting for you to mess up so that she can show him how a REAL woman will treat him. Once again I know this isn't fair, but is life? So when you have found that good man; or in some cases good enough for you . . . take the fight to the world to keep him. I mean, come on now I am by no means an expert in math, but always remember . . . 17 to 1 is crazy and that is what you are fighting with. This number doesn't care about you or your feelings. The women that are sitting out there without a man on every weekend . . . longing to have a person just be there. These same women are looking for a man that will hold them, take them to that movie that you are complaining about . . . that trip to the buffet that you can't stand, you know the one where you roll your eyes every time he mentions it.

It is so simple; a man wants to see you in that sexy mood. It does not mean that he wants to jump your bones every night, but if you know that he has a very high sex drive and you went along at first. Now you don't want to have sex as much . . . . you got a major problem coming. In his mind he is wondering what is going on, damn is she cheating already. Does she not like me anymore, am I pleasing her right, what is going on? Once you let your man start to wonder these things . . . he will seek confirmation that he still got it. Now he will seek this from another woman, but it will take him some time before he really steps out there and tries. He will try with you, and the more you turn him away . . . the closer he gets to see that other woman. All of a sudden he is not over as much, at first it doesn't bother you . . . . hell you need the "Me" time. Now you are missing him and all of the stupid little silly things he used to do. Well, he is over her house . . . because she is giving it up. She is putting him to sleep; she is cooking that meal that you are just too tired to do. She fixes him a plate and brings it to him. All of the little things that you feel too independent to do, she is doing it and doing it well. Since you got on your little 'I can do bad by myself hat' or 'I don't need a man' . . . she is there stroking his ego and she is winning his heart. It is funny reading this; I know so many of you say what you will do when you get that man that God has for you.

As you read what I just said about this . . . in your mind you are trying to figure this out. Think for a minute how many good men you have chased away. For the record I know that some of you have never been in the wrong . . . . it was always his fault . . . blah, blah, blah. Stop pointing the finger . . . I know that there are some guys that made you put down your religion and curse him slap out. Then you pick it up . . . I understand that. What I am talking about . . . is when you had that good man and you let him go because you had this attitude. I don't do this . . . I don't do that. Stop letting other folks tell you how to live your life with that man. Go get your lingerie, and let him know and smell that you care. Remember when he sees sexy, he will look at you. Now if he got this at home his chances are straying go down a lot . . . notice I didn't say that will stop him, all I said is that it will go down.

Try different things to keep his attention . . . don't do the same things that you do to get him. A new perfume . . . a new color in your hair . . . don't let your nails look like you have been digging in the garden, remember that we view you ladies as a thing of beauty make sure it stays that way. We even look to see how the toes are looking. Yes we do that, a lot.

MAGIC BLUE PILLS

Here comes a problem for married women.

That sweet man that loved you for you, he is so attentive to all of your little things. He has been there thru thick and thin, and you have been there with him as well. He started having problems sexually and couldn't get it up . . . you loved him so you stuck it out. It didn't matter that you couldn't have sex as much . . . and when you did have sex it might not have lasted as long. You were happy and contempt with your life, then these fools came out with all of these pills, and now that man is a sex machine. You got two choices with this one, you can get your motor running again or you can let him go out there. The bad thing about letting him go out there is that there are so many diseases out there and if he brings something home to you . . . you might kill him.

If you are ready to go, then you got no problem. Don't worry about this at all. Some ladies have higher sex drives as they get older we all know this . . . heck you might have been sneaking some yourself . . . . but I digress.

Just talk to him and make him understand that your body can't do the things it used to do, the main problem with this is that little hoochie down the street that is trying to get your man to pay a bill or two for his five minutes of fun. Some of you have known your husband have been cheating and you just figure its fine he is taking care of home. Why should I let her get everything I worked to get with him . . . he knows where home is. Girl, please most of that stuff is material. You can replace it . . . can you replace your health if he gives you something a pill or shot can't heal.

I think I would rather have my health and live my life to the fullest, than knowing I got HIV/AIDS because my spouse went out there and cheated and then gave it to me. Now this is the time where I tell you to be selfish, I know it goes against some of the other things I have said earlier but I value marriage and nothing, and I mean nothing should interfere. He should feel the same way and if doesn't then you have to leave him and leave him now . . . the only bad thing is that now you are back at the start of this book. Life just ain't fair is it.

Wrapping this entire thing up!!!!

One moment of thinking, will save six months of Pain!!

One moment of listening, can save you tears later!!!

Take one moment, and you can correct all that you have done . . . it is never too late to start over!!!

I truly hope that what I have given you will help you along this crazy road of dating that we all must take. Now if you are still shaking your head saying "I don't need this" I would advise you to start back over and read it again and this time, open your mind and close your eyes and listen. Once again I have you wondering what do I mean . . . . don't see yourself in the situation ever again and it won't happen. Listen to that thing you ladies have I think you call it "Women's Intuition".

So go ahead start deleting the numbers and forgetting about the good times that you had, and start a new a new day with a smile.

If you follow your gut, you can really knock half of your problems. That's right no matter how smart, how fine, how much money you have, remember that there is always another woman and she could have more.

You will have to deal with this, but now you know that you can have more power or even get back the power you had before.

Remember it is your position to not be used but, understand how all of this can relate to you. I wrote this book not to be hurtful to anyone, but to merely clear the air, because a lot of you are thinking "I AM THE ONE" when you are not. I wrote this book to help those who really wanted to understand, how we (men) really think and how we act. Now I am not saying all men act this way, but for the most part I just got tired of meeting some of the most beautiful ladies in Atlanta and you were still hurting because of what another guy did, I am not him I did not hurt you. I truly understand that you have to heal first, but the first part of that is realizing that you got played and know that with everyday comes a new rising of the Sun and with that you can be a better person. Now if you are saying this has nothing to do with me, I don't get played or used—you are in that 1% of women that are perfect. All of us at one time or another has gotten played or used. Knowledge is power, and power is Knowledge . . . knowing how to use it is half the battle.

As you can now see, I didn't try to fill pages full of psycho mumbo-jumbo. I wanted to give you the meat on the bones and nothing else, with this it makes it clearer for you to see what is going on.

Until next time, I remain peacefully yours

. . . Manswell Peterson Sr.

Printed in the United States
98210LV00005B/328-333/A